A Brief Look at Systems Engineering

Mark Gilbert

Copyright © 2024 Mark Gilbert

All rights reserved.

ISBN: 9798340211330

DEDICATION

I want to dedicate this book to all those engineers who have listened to my ramblings on what I believe systems engineering to be and those who have shaped my understanding in the early years.

More importantly, my long-suffering wife, who has had to listen to me complain repeatedly about the perceptions of systems engineering followed by a lengthy, time-consuming explanation of what systems engineering is and how it should be used

CONTENTS

	Acknowledgements	i
1	Introduction	1
2	General Systems Theory	10
3	The Systems Lifecycle	18
4	Challenges in Systems Engineering	25
5	Challenges and Realising Benefits	33
6	Emerging Trends and the Future	41
7	Conclusion & Outlook	48

ACKNOWLEDGMENTS

I would like to acknowledge the people and organisations below without who I would not understand systems engineering.

1. The Royal Air Force, as they taught me not only how to be a great systems engineer but also how to hold my own in banter.

2. My parents, who carefully looked at me and, after I explained systems engineering, said "No, we still don't know what you do". Hence this book.

3. Metis Europe, who are a great company that has given me a unique perspective on how to apply systems engineering to benefit the customer.

A Brief Look at Systems Engineering

1 INTRODUCTION

I am going to start this whole book with the controversial thought that there is no such thing as "A systems engineer". Before everyone faints and those out there working in this field spit their tea out, hear me through, after all, I have made a good living from selling myself as "a systems engineer". Systems engineering is a mindset and a selection of tools that enable the engineer to look beyond the individual components and instead at the full system as a capability to achieve the end goal.

In general, systems engineering is considered by most technology companies to be a specialised field that integrates multidisciplinary knowledge, advanced methodologies, and complex processes to develop systems, such as aircraft, defence capabilities, spacecraft, satellites, transportation, and Unmanned Aerial Vehicles (UAVs). The discipline focuses on the design, analysis, optimisation, and management of these systems from conception through to operational use.

But I would argue that these disciplines are engineering titles in their own right and as such come under the banner of systems engineering but should not be called systems engineers. It is no different to saying administrator, but what do they do in each role?

Another strange concept that seems to keep being mentioned in my line of work is that systems engineering is specific to a domain. This is a complete myth that is perpetuated by those who do not understand systems engineering. For example, just because it found its main use in aerospace and space does not mean that it cannot be used in health care. Moreover, the person practicing systems engineering does not need to fully understand the specific domain it is used in as the methodologies and theories work in all fields. It is the role of the engineer to bring together multiple specialists to offer the knowledge of the domain and then apply the systems engineering methodologies.

This chapter explores the core theories and methodologies that underpin systems engineering, offering a foundation for understanding the systematic approach necessary for developing and managing such intricate technologies. Some elements are dived into further in this book.

Systems Engineering Overview

At its core, systems engineering is an interdisciplinary field that focuses on designing and managing complex systems over their life cycles. It emphasises a holistic approach to problem-solving, ensuring that each component of a system works seamlessly within the broader framework. Not forgetting that there is the ability to have systems within systems, or a Systems of Systems (SoS).

Within this book, I have focused examples on the aerospace application of systems engineering to provide examples, although you should keep in mind this is only as the aerospace sector amplifies this complexity due to its stringent safety requirements, high-performance demands, and cross-domain nature, encompassing mechanical, electrical, software, thermal, and human factors (there are many more). Systems engineering is responsible for ensuring that each of these diverse elements is integrated effectively, leading to the successful realisation of highly complex and often mission-critical systems.

I cannot emphasise enough that systems engineering is domain-agnostic. Systems engineering focuses on several key objectives:

- **Safety and Reliability:** Systems, especially those involving human life, must meet rigorous safety and reliability standards.

- **Performance Optimisation:** This is especially important for air or maritime platforms as they need to be efficient, sometimes fast, and capable of withstanding extreme environments.

- **Integration of Technologies:** Modern systems involve the integration of advanced technologies from various fields, for example, aerospace includes propulsion, avionics (**AVI**ation electr**ONICS**), communications, and materials science.

- **Lifecycle Management:** Managing the entire lifecycle of the system, from conceptual design to disposal or decommissioning, is a critical focus and is the core focus of systems engineering.

Methodology in Systems Engineering

The methodology of systems engineering follows a structured, process-oriented approach. These methodologies are often standardised, such as the one developed by the International Council on Systems Engineering (INCOSE) and adapted to the specific needs of complex projects. Systems engineering is often carried out in a particular order and follows what is called the V-cycle.

It is a matter of discussion whether the first step is capturing and defining the system's requirements or defining the concept. Either way, both need to happen at the beginning as it is both that define what the system is, how and where it is used, who uses it, and what it needs to have in order to achieve the end goal. The processes are defined as:

Requirements Engineering – many complex systems have stringent requirements driven by regulatory standards (such as those from the Federal Aviation Authority (FAA) US Aviation, Civil Aviation Authority (CAA) UK aviation, and Military Aviation Authority (MAA) for UK defence), environmental constraints, and user needs. This phase involves the meticulous documentation of performance criteria, safety protocols, mission objectives, and operational constraints. Requirements are typically divided into:

- **Functional requirements** (what must it do)
- **Non-functional requirements** (how it must do it)
- **Interface requirements** (how does it interact with other systems)

Conceptual Design and Feasibility Analysis - Conceptual design explores the multitude of ways the system can be designed so that it meets the defined objectives. Remember there is always more than one way to skin a cat. Engineers use experience combined with modelling and simulation tools and methods to assess the feasibility of the different concepts, these can include structural design, power system choices (battery vs combustion), and communication architectures. Trade studies are conducted to compare the relative benefits of different design choices, such as the use of specific materials, power sources, or communication protocols.

System Architecture and Decomposition - Once the design is selected, usually through many design reviews that can take a long time, the system is decomposed into smaller, more manageable subsystems. For aerospace systems, this decomposition might include propulsion, avionics, communications, entertainment, and structural components. These subsystems can then be broken down into individual components and elements if the subsystem is still relatively large in complexity. Systems engineering is all about reducing complexity.

Each subsystem can be either engineered in parallel, but with continual communication between the engineers, or one at a time if integration is not too complex, for example, if the size of a car seat is known the exact design is not as important when designing the size of the interior of a car. A significant aspect of systems engineering is managing these interfaces and ensuring the flow of data, power, and control signals between the different subsystems.

At the end of this exercise, we will have a complete set of architectural designs, or as my friend says, "a load of pretty pictures with boxes all over it", that will give a picture of what each part does, how it integrates with the whole, and what technology capabilities are needed. These can be used in future upgrades to provide a capability gap analysis and impact statement when removing one box to insert a new one. It is a powerful tool when used correctly, but it is important to remember it is simply this and the advantage lies with the correct use of the tool by a skilled individual.

Model-Based Systems Engineering (MBSE) - MBSE is the latest buzzword in aerospace and defence systems engineering. This methodology relies on digital models to represent every aspect of the system's architecture, design, analysis, and verification. MBSE generally allows for greater accuracy and traceability in complex projects and helps to visualise how subsystems will interact throughout the system's lifecycle. MBSE is covered more later in the book.

Verification and Validation (V&V) - Verification and validation ensure that the system meets the requirements and functions as expected in real-world scenarios. This process is especially critical in aerospace and maritime applications due to the extreme environmental conditions and high reliability required.

This is where verification comes in and typically occurs on bench testing or in simulated environments, wind tunnels, and Hardware-In-Loop (HIL) tests. The testing can be automated through test scripts and large banks of test equipment or can simply be a human turning a switch on and off at pre-defined points in the test. While validation occurs in real-world tests, such as flight tests for aircraft or launch trials. Developing the trials programmes can come under the banner of systems engineering.

Lifecycle Management & Continuous Improvement - Systems must be managed throughout their lifecycle, from the initial concept through to development, deployment, maintenance, and eventual retirement. Lifecycle management ensures that systems remain operationally viable and can be upgraded or retrofitted as needed. Engineers using systems engineering methods play a crucial role in ensuring that updates and modifications do not introduce new risks or degrade system performance.

Core Theoretical Framework

The theory behind systems engineering is built on the principles of general systems theory, control theory, and optimisation. These foundational concepts allow engineers to manage the complexity inherent in modern systems, ensuring they meet predefined performance, safety, and operational goals.

General Systems Theory - This theory emphasises that the whole system is greater than the sum of its parts. Think of a jigsaw puzzle. Every piece has a part of the picture on it, but it is only when put in the right place that the full picture is revealed. In aerospace, this means that every component, whether it's a propulsion unit, a control system, or a structural element, must be designed not only to meet its specific individual requirements but to function within the larger context of the entire system to achieve the overall goal. The interactions between subsystems are as, if not more, important than the subsystems themselves. There is a lot of work carried out to make sure these interactions are not only working but are fully documented for future improvements or technology insertions.

Control Theory - Control theory is often carried out under systems engineering and is essential for predicting, monitoring, and managing the dynamic behaviour of the system. It provides the mathematical framework for understanding how systems respond to external inputs and how to ensure they maintain desired performance over time. Aerospace systems for example, such as autopilot controls or satellite attitude management, rely heavily on robust control systems to ensure a high level of stability and precision in extremely dynamic environments.

Optimisation Theory - Optimisation theory deals with improving system performance subject to certain constraints, such as weight, cost, and energy efficiency. Once the system has been designed at the concept stage it is here that the system is refined and improved upon through trade-off studies, whilst still achieving the final goal. Systems engineering often requires the balancing of conflicting requirements. For instance, minimising the weight of an aircraft might negatively impact structural integrity, so the challenge is to find optimal trade-offs between performance criteria. Sometimes a requirement is so conflicted that it cannot be met. In this case, it is down to the authorising team to decide if this requirement is critical or can be removed altogether. For example, if I were to have two requirements, one to have a TV in the bedroom and another to put in a wardrobe but both are to be put in the same available space this would be conflicting and so I would need to decide which is the more vital, TV or wardrobe and so only one requirement can be met.

Emerging Trends and the Future of Systems Engineering

The future of systems engineering is evolving rapidly due to advancements in automation, artificial intelligence, and autonomous systems. Each one of these adds more and more complexity. In the past systems engineering and software engineering were treated as two very separate entities, never to talk to each other. Now it is almost impossible to look at the system without the consideration of software and vice versa. In fact, in software engineering, they have a new skill in constant demand called DevOps. This is just systems engineering by any other name.

The main key trends coming through in many different engineering fields include:

- **Autonomous Systems:** In aerospace, this is in the form of Unmanned Aerial Vehicles (UAVs), but it is also heavily researched in transportation and manufacturing. Systems are becoming more autonomous, requiring sophisticated control algorithms and sensor integration.

- **Digital Twins:** The development of Digital Twins, virtual replicas of physical systems, enables real-time monitoring and optimisation of complex systems, enhancing predictive maintenance and reducing downtime. Essentially this is a simulation on the computer that represents what is happening in the real world, but as data from the real world is gathered it is fed back into the model to improve it. The theory is that eventually, the simulation will behave the same as the real world.

- **Sustainability and Green Engineering:** There is a growing focus on designing systems that are more energy-efficient, sustainable, and capable of operating in environmentally responsible ways, such as using alternative fuels or developing reusable materials.

Challenges in Systems Engineering

Systems engineering, along with almost every other domain, faces unique challenges compared to other engineering fields. Some of these are:

- **Integration of Cutting-Edge Technologies:** For example, the aerospace industry constantly pushes the boundaries of technology. Integrating new materials, propulsion technologies, autonomous control systems, and AI-driven decision-making processes presents a constant challenge.

- **Stringent Safety Standards:** Systems must be designed to operate safely under extreme conditions such as high or low temperatures, pressures, or speeds. As new standards are introduced, for example, regarding the use of AI, it is a constant battle within systems engineering to ensure the system's compliance with those standards that are relevant but ever-changing.

- **Cost and Schedule Constraints:** Complex projects are often constrained by tight budgets and schedules. Engineers must balance these constraints while delivering high-quality, reliable systems. This is more of a challenge in modern times where the cost of products and services is on the rise at a rapid rate. In defence, for example, the need for a system to be deployed instantly into the hands of the soldier is always contrary to the time needed ideally to conduct perfect systems engineering.

- **Environmental Concerns:** All sectors are increasingly focused on reducing their environmental impact, this means engineering needs to innovate technology for efficiency, emissions reduction, materials recycling, and so on. Governments are committing to net zero deadlines and industries are being pressured to comply.

2 GENERAL SYSTEMS THEORY

General Systems Theory provides the foundation for understanding how complex systems function and interact. The concept as we know it now was developed by an Austrian biologist called Ludwig von Bertalanffy in the mid-20th century (although the Soviet Alexander Bogdanov theorised general systems in the 1920s). Who developed it is not important for this book, except if you find yourself in a pub quiz and asked about general systems theory. As we all love a good acronym, we shall call it 'GST'. It offers a framework that has no specific domain but rather applies to a wide range of fields, from biology and social science to engineering and industry. GST enables engineers to conceptualise, design, and manage any highly complex system. This chapter explores GST in more depth, highlighting its key principles and its application to the real world.

Foundations of General Systems Theory

At its core, GST is built on the premise that systems should be understood as a whole, not merely as collections of independent parts. A system is defined as a set of interrelated components that work together to achieve a common goal. The theory emphasises the connection between these components and the relationships that emerge between them. Think of a rugby team where each player has a role but unless they work as a team then there is no way that the club will win anything.

In aerospace engineering, an aircraft is not simply a sum of its individual subsystems such as propulsion, avionics, and structures but a complex network between them. GST provides the theoretical basis to model and manage these interactions.

The key components of General Systems Theory are:

- **Holism:** Systems must be understood in totality, where the behaviour of the system emerges from the interaction of its parts.

- **Hierarchy:** Systems are often composed of subsystems, which in turn may consist of smaller elements, creating hierarchical structures.

- **Homeostasis and Stability:** Systems have mechanisms to maintain equilibrium and ensure stable operation, despite external disturbances.

- **Feedback Loops:** Feedback processes, both positive and negative, influence how systems react to changes in the environment or within the system itself.

- **Open Systems:** Most systems are open, meaning they exchange energy, information, or even physical material with their external environment.

Holism and System Integration

Holism is the principle that the whole is greater than the sum of its parts. This is particularly important in aerospace systems, where the interactions between subsystems can determine the overall performance and safety of the aircraft. For example, a well-designed propulsion system is ineffective if the airframe cannot support the stresses induced by the generated thrust. There is nothing worse than seeing the, no longer attached, engine fly past the cockpit window.

In aerospace engineering, achieving an integrated, holistic design requires a deep understanding of how different components affect one another. A change in one subsystem can have cascading effects throughout the system. For example, reducing the weight of an aircraft's structure may increase fuel efficiency, but could compromise the vehicle's structural integrity, requiring compensatory design changes in other areas. Engineers working on the systems level must therefore consider the entire system in their design approach, rather than optimising individual components in isolation. As already mentioned this means that the engineer, when carrying out systems engineering, needs to understand elements of all parts. This does not mean that they are experts in all disciplines, but rather they are good at extracting information from those who are the experts in each field.

This holistic view is essential for:

- **System Optimisation:** Ensuring that the performance of individual components contributes to the overall performance goals of the system.

- **Interoperability:** Guaranteeing that subsystems can communicate and function together, especially in aerospace systems where integration of avionics, communications, propulsion, and control systems is critical.

- **Safety and Reliability:** Understanding how failures in one part of the system can propagate through the whole and designing to mitigate risks at the system level. Remember systems engineering is all about reducing risk.

Hierarchical Systems and Subsystem Decomposition

Another core concept of General Systems Theory is hierarchy, where complex systems are organised into layers of subsystems, each of which can be further broken down into smaller elements. In aerospace systems, hierarchy allows engineers to manage complexity by breaking down large systems into manageable units.

For example, if we look at the power supply system on the aircraft, we can have the following hierarchy (I understand this is neither exhaustive nor complete):

- **Power Supply System**
    - AC Power System
        - AC Generation
            - Ground Power System
            - Main Engine 1 Power System
        - AC Control
            - Monitoring
            - Fault
        - AC Distribution………

I am sure you get the idea and if you were to look at these systems on an actual aircraft you will find that there are volumes of books (or computer chapters now) dedicated to these systems. In aerospace, these are broken down into ATA chapters (Air Transport Association) of which there are 100 chapters, some spanning more than one book.

Hierarchical decomposition enables:

- **Modularity:** Subsystems can be designed, tested, and refined independently before being integrated into the overall system. This simplifies the development process and allows different teams to work on different subsystems simultaneously.

- **Traceability (not requirements):** Engineers can track the flow of energy, data, and control through the system, from the highest-level system (e.g., platform) down to the smallest components (e.g., sensors).

- **Fault Isolation:** If a fault occurs, engineers can trace it to a specific subsystem or component, rather than having to troubleshoot the entire system. I was always taught the split system method where you test at the system mid-point and see which side the fault occurs and so on until it is located.

Homeostasis and Stability in Complex Systems

Homeostasis refers to a system's ability to maintain stability and function under varying conditions. In aerospace systems, maintaining stability is crucial, particularly in dynamic environments such as space or high-altitude flight, where external conditions are unpredictable.

For example, an aircraft's autopilot system is designed to maintain stable flight by continuously adjusting control surfaces in response to changing airspeed, altitude, and weather conditions. Similarly, a spacecraft's thermal control system ensures that internal temperatures remain within a safe range, despite external fluctuations in solar radiation or atmospheric conditions.

In these cases, systems must be designed with feedback mechanisms that detect deviations from desired conditions and take corrective action. For aerospace systems, stability is often achieved through:

- **Control Systems:** Autonomous systems that continuously monitor and adjust system performance, such as autopilot or satellite attitude control systems.
- **Redundancy:** Multiple layers of redundancy ensure that critical functions can continue, even if one component fails. For example, spacecraft typically have multiple communication channels to ensure that contact can be maintained with mission control in case of an antenna or transmitter failure.
- **Safety Margins:** Systems are designed with wide safety margins, ensuring that even if environmental conditions exceed expected limits, the system will remain functional.

Feedback Loops: Positive and Negative Feedback

Feedback is a fundamental concept in systems theory, referring to the process where a system's output is fed back into the system as input, influencing future behaviour. There are two main types of feedback:

- **Negative Feedback:** This stabilises systems by reducing deviations from a desired state. For instance, an aircraft's autopilot uses negative feedback to maintain a stable altitude. When the aircraft drifts above or below the desired altitude, the system automatically adjusts control surfaces to bring the aircraft back to the set altitude. Negative feedback helps maintain homeostasis and prevent runaway conditions.

- **Positive Feedback:** This amplifies changes, potentially leading to exponential growth or system instability. In aerospace, positive feedback can occur in undesirable situations, such as when aerodynamic forces cause an aircraft to enter a stall. If not counteracted, the stall can worsen due to increasing drag and decreasing lift. Positive feedback often requires robust control systems to prevent uncontrolled escalation.

Feedback loops are essential for dynamic system control, especially in the unpredictable environments encountered in aerospace engineering. Engineers design systems with feedback loops that allow the system to respond appropriately to changes and disturbances, ensuring stable and predictable performance.

Open Systems and Environmental Interaction

Most systems are open systems, meaning they interact with their environment by exchanging energy, matter, or information. For instance, an aircraft exchanges energy with the atmosphere in the form of lift, drag, and heat. A satellite in orbit exchanges information with ground stations through electromagnetic signals.

Understanding these interactions is crucial for design engineers because the performance of the system is often heavily influenced by external environmental factors. In designing open systems, engineers must consider:

- **Environmental Forces:** Aircraft and spacecraft are subjected to environmental forces such as gravity, atmospheric pressure, and wind. These forces affect flight dynamics and structural integrity.

- **Energy Management:** Managing energy exchange, such as heat dissipation in spacecraft or fuel efficiency in aircraft, is critical for ensuring long-term operability.

- **Signal Exchange:** Systems rely on communication systems to send and receive data, often over vast distances. Engineers must account for signal attenuation, interference, and delays, especially in space missions. Not forgetting that data security is more vital now than ever before.

Designing systems that can operate effectively within these open environments is a core challenge in systems engineering. The system must be resilient, adaptable, and capable of maintaining stability in the face of external perturbations.

Application of General Systems Theory in Complex Projects

General Systems Theory is applied throughout the systems engineering process, from conceptual design to operations. Key applications include:

- **System Modelling and Simulation:** GST provides a framework for creating models and simulations of complex systems, allowing engineers to predict system behaviour before physical prototypes are built. This is particularly important in aerospace, where testing in real-world environments (e.g., space) is expensive and time-consuming.

- **Interdisciplinary Coordination:** GST fosters a multidisciplinary approach, encouraging collaboration between different engineering teams. Engineers practising systems engineering act as coordinators, ensuring that mechanical, electrical, software and human factors are integrated into a cohesive design.

- **Risk Management:** GST allows for better identification and management of risks, particularly those that arise from subsystem interactions or external environmental factors.

Chapter Conclusion

General Systems Theory provides a powerful framework for understanding and managing the complexity of systems. Its principles of holism, hierarchy, feedback, and openness guide engineers in designing systems that are not only technically sophisticated but also robust, reliable, and adaptable to changing environments. By applying these concepts, engineers are better equipped to tackle the challenges of creating high-performance systems capable of withstanding the extreme conditions of flight and space exploration.

3 THE SYSTEMS ENGINEERING LIFECYCLE

In general, systems are highly complex, requiring a structured and disciplined approach to their design, development, and operation. One of the most effective ways to manage this complexity is through the **Systems Engineering Lifecycle**, a step-by-step framework that guides engineers from the early conceptual stages to the retirement of a system. Each phase of this lifecycle employs specific methodologies to ensure the system meets its requirements efficiently and effectively. In this chapter, we will explore the key methodologies used during each phase of the Systems Engineering Lifecycle, breaking down complex engineering concepts so both engineers and non-engineers can understand the processes involved. The most common framework is the V-cycle that guides the engineer through the lifecycle steps with the start being at the top left of the V and ending at the top right. As you move down the left side you are developing and designing the system. Then as you move up the right side you are testing and proving the design. I believe it should be more of a circle as once it is designed you do not forget about it but go through the same process for new tech or upgrades/fixes. This simple process is explained below.

Conceptual Design Phase (Top Left)

The Conceptual Design phase is the first stage in the lifecycle, where the initial ideas and basic framework for the system are developed. During this phase, engineers work to define the broad goals and constraints of the system, exploring different approaches and solutions.

Key Methodologies are:

- **Requirements Analysis:** One of the first tasks in this phase is identifying the needs and expectations of the system's users or stakeholders. This involves interviews, workshops, and market research to gather requirements. Once gathered, engineers organise these into technical specifications.
    - **Example**: In the case of designing a new aircraft, requirements analysis might involve specifying the range, speed, fuel efficiency, and safety features expected by airlines and regulatory bodies.

- **Trade-off Studies**: Early in the design process, there are often multiple possible solutions to the same problem. Trade-off studies compare these options based on criteria such as cost, performance, and feasibility. This process helps ensure that the best solution is chosen before moving on to more detailed design work.
    - **Example**: Deciding between different materials for the aircraft's fuselage, balancing weight versus cost and durability.

- **Feasibility Analysis**: Engineers assess whether the proposed designs and technologies are practical and achievable within the project's budget and time constraints. This analysis might involve simulations, basic models, or the use of experience.

Preliminary Design Phase

Once a concept is chosen, the next step is the Preliminary Design phase, where the system's architecture begins to take shape. Engineers start defining the subsystems and components, and more detailed designs are created.

Key Methodologies are:

- **Modelling and Simulation**: In this phase, engineers use computer models and simulations to predict how the system will behave under various conditions. These models allow for the early identification of potential issues without the need to build costly prototypes.

    o **Example**: Simulating the aerodynamics of an aircraft wing to predict how it will perform in different weather conditions or altitudes.

- **System Architecture Development**: System architecture is essentially the blueprint for how different subsystems will interact with one another. It ensures that all the components, from engines to avionics, work together harmoniously.

    o **Example**: Developing an architecture that integrates the aircraft's control systems, propulsion, and navigation systems.

- **Risk Analysis**: This methodology focuses on identifying potential risks early in the design process. Engineers assess the likelihood of each risk and its potential impact on the project. Based on this, they develop strategies to mitigate against or manage these risks.

Detailed Design Phase

In the Detailed Design phase, the system is fleshed out in full detail. Every subsystem and component are designed, and precise engineering drawings are created. At this stage, engineers aim to finalise the design and ensure that everything is ready for production or manufacturing.

Key Methodologies are:

- **Optimisation Techniques**: As the system design becomes more detailed, optimisation methodologies are used to refine the performance of specific components. These techniques can help reduce weight, improve fuel efficiency, or minimise costs. Various types of optimisation methods are employed, including gradient-based techniques for continuous systems and genetic algorithms, a method for solving constrained and unconstrained problems that are based on natural selection, for more complex, non-linear problems.
    - **Example**: Optimising the shape of a wing to reduce drag and improve fuel efficiency without compromising structural integrity.

- **Finite Element Analysis (FEA)**: FEA is a computational technique used to predict how components will behave under stress, strain, and other physical forces. This ensures that the system's parts will withstand the operational conditions they will face.
    - **Example**: Using FEA to predict how the aircraft fuselage will handle turbulence or extreme temperature variations.

- **Prototyping**: In some cases, a physical or virtual prototype of the system or its components is built. This allows engineers to test the system in simulated real-world conditions, providing valuable feedback before moving into the manufacturing phase.

Integration and Testing Phase

Once the detailed design is complete, the system components are manufactured or developed and then integrated into a complete system. This is followed by rigorous testing to ensure the system functions as expected.

Key Methodologies are:

- **System Integration**: This methodology focuses on combining the different subsystems (e.g., avionics, propulsion, control systems) into a fully functioning system. It requires careful coordination to ensure that all parts work together without conflicts or failures.

    o **Example**: Integrating an aircraft's flight control system with its navigation and communication systems to ensure smooth operation.

- **Verification and Validation (V&V)**: Verification ensures that the system has been built according to its specifications, while validation checks that the system meets the needs of its users. These processes involve a combination of simulations, physical tests, and reviews.

    o **Example**: Testing the flight performance of a new aircraft in a wind tunnel, followed by actual flight tests to confirm it meets safety standards.

- **Performance Testing**: Once the system is integrated, it is subjected to performance tests to see how well it meets the objectives defined in the requirements phase. This might include tests for speed, fuel efficiency, stability, and more.

Operation and Maintenance Phase (Top Right)

After the system has been developed and tested, it enters the operational phase. During this phase, the system is used in its intended environment, and maintenance activities are carried out to ensure it remains in good working condition.

Key Methodologies are:

- **Maintenance and Reliability Engineering**: Engineers develop strategies for maintaining the system over its operational life. This includes routine checks, repairs, and replacements to prevent unexpected failures. Reliability engineering is used to predict the likelihood of component failures and plan maintenance schedules accordingly.
    - **Example**: The scheduling of regular maintenance checks on an aircraft's engines and control systems to ensure they function reliably throughout their service life.
- **System Monitoring and Feedback Loops**: During operation, data from the system is continuously monitored to assess performance and identify any potential issues. Feedback loops allow engineers to adjust and make improvements based on real-world data.
    - **Example**: Using real-time flight data to monitor fuel efficiency and engine performance, allowing for adjustments to improve performance.

Decommissioning and Disposal Phase

The final stage of the lifecycle is decommissioning and disposal, where the system is retired after its operational life. This phase requires careful planning to safely and responsibly dispose of the system or its components.

Key Methodologies are:

- **Decommissioning Planning**: Engineers plan how the system will be safely taken out of service. This might involve dismantling components, disposing of hazardous materials, and/or repurposing parts for other uses.
    - **Example**: Decommissioning an aircraft and recycling its materials or converting its components for use in training simulators. Airbus even made shoes and bags out of aisle carpet.

- **Environmental Impact Assessment**: Systems, particularly large-scale ones like aircraft or satellites, can have significant environmental impacts when decommissioned. Engineers assess the environmental effects of disposal and develop methods to minimise them, such as recycling or safe disposal of hazardous materials.
    - **Example**: Safely disposing of fuel and toxic chemicals from an old aircraft to minimise environmental damage.

Chapter Conclusion

The Systems Engineering Lifecycle provides a structured approach to developing complex systems, ensuring they meet performance, safety, and regulatory requirements. By applying different methodologies at each stage of the lifecycle, engineers can optimise design, reduce risks, and create high-performing systems that operate reliably throughout their lifespan. Whether in the conceptual phase or during decommissioning, each methodology plays a critical role in the success of any complex system.

4 CHALLENGES IN SYSTEMS ENGINEERING

As we have already stated systems engineering involves the development and management of highly complex systems, where, amongst other things, precision, reliability, and safety are paramount. However, the field is not without its challenges. From the very beginning when you are developing the product/capability these challenges span from technological hurdles to regulatory constraints, the path to creating successful systems is fraught with obstacles. In this chapter we explore the main challenges faced across systems engineering, focusing again on examples from aerospace systems engineering due to its high level of complexity, but these can be applied in other industries with ease. Here we are providing a detailed look at each issue to help both engineers and non-engineers understand the complexities involved.

Complexity of Systems

Systems are intrinsically intricate in the modern world, consisting of many subsystems and components that must function together harmoniously. This complexity stems from the integration of diverse technologies, adherence to strict performance standards, and the necessity for safety and reliability.

Key Methodologies are:

- **Integration of Subsystems**: Systems often consist of multiple subsystems, for example in aerospace there are propulsion, avionics, and structural components. Ensuring that these subsystems integrate correctly is a huge challenge and a key role in systems engineering.
    - **Example**: Integrating a new avionics system with an existing propulsion system requires careful coordination to ensure that the two systems communicate effectively and do not cause any conflicts.
- **Design and Testing**: Designing and testing complex systems involves creating models and prototypes, running simulations, and conducting real-world tests. The complexity of these processes means that even small errors can have significant consequences.
    - **Example**: A small error in the design of an aircraft wing could lead to major issues in flight performance, necessitating extensive testing and potential redesign.

Impact on Methodologies:

- **System Engineering Practices**: Engineers must use advanced systems engineering practices to manage complexity, including rigorous design reviews, integration testing, and Model-Based Systems Engineering (MBSE).
- **Risk Management**: Managing the risks associated with system complexity requires thorough risk assessments, robust testing protocols, and contingency planning.

High Costs and Budget Constraints

Complex engineering projects often involve substantial financial investment, from research and development to production and maintenance. Budget constraints can limit the scope of projects and affect the quality and performance of the final system.

Key Methodologies are:

- **Research and Development (R&D)**: The R&D phase is particularly costly, involving the development of new technologies, materials, and designs. Budget constraints can limit the extent of experimentation and innovation.

   o **Example**: Developing a new type of fuel-efficient engine requires significant investment in research, testing, and validation, which may be constrained by available funds.

- **Production and Manufacturing**: Manufacturing systems involve high precision and specialised processes, which are often expensive. Cost overruns can occur due to unforeseen issues or changes in design requirements.

   o **Example**: If unexpected issues arise during the production of an aircraft, additional costs may be incurred to resolve these issues and ensure the final product meets quality standards.

Impact on Methodologies:

- **Cost-Effective Design**: Engineers must balance performance and cost, often opting for design solutions that maximise value while staying within budget constraints.

- **Lifecycle Cost Management**: Effective management of lifecycle costs, including maintenance and operational costs, is crucial for ensuring long-term financial viability.

Regulatory and Compliance Issues

Regulations are extensive in the systems world and must be complied with. For example, the aerospace industry is highly regulated, with strict standards and regulations governing every aspect of system design, production, and operation. Compliance with these regulations is essential but can be challenging due to their complexity and the evolving nature of regulatory requirements.

Key Methodologies are:

- **Safety Standards**: Systems must meet rigorous safety standards to protect passengers, crew, and cargo. Compliance with these standards requires thorough testing and documentation.
    - **Example**: Aircraft must undergo extensive certification processes to ensure they meet safety requirements, including tests for structural integrity, avionics performance, and emergency systems.

- **Environmental Regulations**: There are increasing demands for systems to minimise their environmental impact. Compliance with regulations on emissions, noise, and waste management requires innovative solutions and may affect system design.
    - **Example**: New regulations may require the development of quieter engines or more fuel-efficient designs to reduce environmental impact.

Impact on Methodologies:

- **Regulatory Compliance**: Engineers must stay updated with current regulations and integrate compliance requirements into the design and testing processes.

- **Documentation and Certification**: Thorough documentation and rigorous testing are essential for meeting certification requirements and ensuring regulatory compliance.

Technological Advancements and Integration

The rapid pace of technological advancements presents both opportunities and challenges in systems engineering. Integrating new technologies into existing systems and ensuring their compatibility can be complex and resource intensive.

Key Methodologies are:

- **Integration of New Technologies**: As new technologies, such as advanced materials or electronic systems become available, integrating them into existing systems requires careful planning and testing.

    o **Example**: Putting a new electrified train onto older tacks may need a full upgrade to the infrastructure.

- **Keeping Up with Innovation**: Staying abreast of technological advancements and incorporating them into systems is crucial for maintaining competitive advantage and meeting evolving performance requirements. The engineer needs to find this new tech and then, if applicable, develop the road map to inserting this technology.

    o **Example**: Manufacturing companies must continually assess and adopt new technologies, such as AI or additive manufacturing, to stay at the forefront of innovation.

Impact on Methodologies:

- **Continuous Improvement**: Engineers must adopt practices that allow continuous improvement and integration of new technologies, including agile development processes and iterative testing.

- **Horizon Scanning**: Identifying and evaluating emerging technologies is essential for making informed decisions about their integration into existing systems.

- **Road Mapping**: Once the technology has been identified and evaluated it needs to be included in the capability road map. If one does not exist, then the engineer should develop one that allows new technology to be inserted at various pre-determined stages (technology drops).

Safety and Reliability Challenges

Ensuring the safety and reliability of critical systems is paramount, given the potential consequences of failures, just ask a well-known aircraft manufacturer about this. Engineers must design systems that can potentially withstand extreme conditions, and constant use, whilst operating reliably over their entire lifecycle.

Key aspects are:

- **Failure Analysis and Prevention**: Identifying potential failure modes and implementing strategies to prevent them is critical. This involves conducting a thorough analysis, including Fault Tree Analysis (FTA) and Failure Modes and Effects Analysis (FMEA).
    - **Example**: Analysing potential failure modes in an aircraft's hydraulic system and implementing redundant systems to prevent failures.

- **Operational Reliability**: Ensuring that systems perform reliably during operation requires rigorous testing, including simulations and field tests, to verify performance under real-world conditions.
    - **Example**: A new point of sale system will undergo full testing if this fails in the real world the supermarket can lose millions in sales (this happened to a supermarket chain one Christmas, and they lost nearly 12 million over 4 hours.

Impact on Methodologies:

- **Safety Engineering**: Engineers must incorporate safety engineering principles into the design process, including redundancy, fault tolerance, and robust testing.

- **Reliability Testing**: Comprehensive reliability testing is essential to ensure that systems meet operational requirements and maintain high performance throughout their lifecycle.

Supply Chain and Manufacturing Challenges

Industry regularly relies on a complex global supply chain, and managing this supply chain effectively is critical for ensuring timely production and delivery of systems. Challenges in supply chain management can impact cost, quality, and delivery schedules.

Key aspects are:

- **Supplier Management**: Ensuring that suppliers meet quality standards and deliver components on time is crucial. Supply chain disruptions or quality issues can have significant impacts on the overall project.
  - **Example**: A delay in the delivery of critical components can halt production and affect project timelines. It is for this reason that some aircraft manufacturers have policies that direct them to look after their suppliers.

- **Manufacturing Processes**: Manufacturing involves complex processes and precision requirements. Managing these processes effectively and addressing issues such as defects or production delays is essential for maintaining quality.
  - **Example**: Ensuring that manufacturing processes for an aircraft's fuselage meet stringent quality standards to avoid defects that could affect performance or safety.

Impact on Methodologies:

- **Supply Chain Management**: Effective supply chain management practices, including supplier selection, quality control, and logistics planning, are essential for minimising disruptions and ensuring timely delivery.

- **Lean Manufacturing**: Implementing lean manufacturing techniques can help optimise production processes, reduce waste, and improve efficiency.

Chapter Conclusion

The challenges in systems engineering are diverse and complex, ranging from managing system complexity and costs to ensuring safety and integrating new technologies. Addressing these challenges requires a combination of advanced engineering practices, innovative solutions, and effective management strategies. By understanding these challenges in detail, engineers and stakeholders can better navigate the complexities of systems engineering and contribute to the development of successful, high-performing systems. It is also worth noting here that many managers and bean counters see the cost of implementing systems engineering at the start as unnecessary and expensive. However, the cost of fixing issues later, which could have been foreseen, is a lot more expensive. Systems engineering is all about reducing risk but is often used to fix the problem when the risk is realised.

5 CHALLENGES AND REALISING BENEFITS

Systems engineering, when executed effectively, is designed to tackle the host of challenges faced by various industries. By employing robust methodologies and innovative approaches, engineers can address the complexities, costs, and other issues inherent in developing advanced systems. It is a strong understanding of these methodologies and their application in the real world that makes systems engineering valuable. Now, books such as this one or the INCOSE SEBOK are a good starting point but should never replace experience. Many engineers pass the exams and say they are systems engineers, but as I have said throughout, firstly a systems engineer does not truly exist, and secondly the complex systems in the real world, unfortunately, do not follow a book, especially when they go wrong and so we need to adapt and tailor the principals. The art of doing this only comes with experience and this is your most powerful tool. Having said all that if you have yet to gain experience then the principals are a good starting point. In this chapter, I try to show how the proper application of systems engineering principles can overcome the challenges outlined in the previous chapter and highlight the benefits that result from successful implementation.

Mitigating Complexity through Structured Processes

Systems engineering offers structured processes to manage and mitigate the inherent complexity of modern systems. These processes ensure that all subsystems and components integrate seamlessly, reducing the risk of conflicts and ensuring that performance requirements are met.

Key Strategies:

- **Model-Based Systems Engineering (MBSE)**: MBSE provides a highly powerful framework for creating comprehensive models of the systems, allowing engineers to visualise, analyse, and manage complex interactions among subsystems. Tools, such as SysML (Systems Modelling Language), are commonly used to map out the system's architecture and track the evolution of requirements through design, testing, and implementation. However, as with the systems architecture methods, it is important not to use these tools just because everyone else is. They should always be able to answer the main questions and not be for the sake of having pretty pictures.
    - **Benefit**: This approach helps in identifying integration issues early, reducing the risk of costly late-stage changes. But remember the model is only as good as the engineer that creates it and the data that is inserted.

- **System Architecture and Design**: A well-defined system architecture lays out the relationships and interactions between subsystems, providing a clear blueprint for integration and development. It can be updated as new technology is inserted. You should never just do architecture for architecture's sake.
    - **Benefit**: The primary benefit of developing a systems architecture model is that it can show the system in a diagram form that is easy to understand for all involved independent of

whether they are engineers or not. A clear architecture reduces the risk of misalignment between subsystems and ensures that all components work together as intended. But it is worth remembering that the architecture will answer a particular question and if used in the wrong context can end up being just a collection of diagrams with no benefit at all.

Resulting Benefits:

- **Reduced Development Time**: Structured processes and early identification of issues lead to faster development cycles and more efficient design iterations.

- **Enhanced Reliability**: A comprehensive approach to system design and integration improves the reliability and performance of the final system.

- **Goal Alignment:** Through a robust structured process everyone will end up on the same page with a clear understanding of the goal and how to get there making the process as efficient as possible.

Managing Costs with Efficient Practices

Effective systems engineering employs various strategies to manage and optimise costs throughout the lifecycle of a system, from initial development to maintenance and end-of-life.

Key Strategies:

- **Cost-Effective Design and Prototyping**: By using advanced simulation tools, such as Digital Twins, engineers can test designs virtually, reducing the need for expensive physical prototypes. By the time the physical tests are carried out most design flaws have already been rectified.

    o **Benefit**: Lower costs in design and prototyping phases, allowing for more iterative and cost-effective development.

- **Lifecycle Cost Management**: Engineers can employ Lifecycle Cost Analysis (LCA) to evaluate the total cost of ownership, including initial costs, maintenance, and operational expenses.
  - **Benefit**: A more informed decision-making that balances initial investment for the cost of the technology with the cost of operating the technology throughout its life. For example, over a 10-year operational use, the most expensive equipment may be the cheapest option overall.

Resulting Benefits:

- **Optimised Budget Allocation**: Efficient management of costs allows for better allocation of resources, reducing financial strain and improving project feasibility.

- **Increased Value**: Cost-effective practices enhance the value of the final system by providing a better balance between performance and expenditure.

Ensuring Compliance with Rigorous Standards

Systems engineering incorporates rigorous compliance checks and standards throughout the design and development process to meet regulatory requirements and ensure safety. This has been increasingly more complex with the advancements in AI integration and cyber threats.

Key Strategies:

- **Integrated Compliance Management**: Systems engineering practices include integrating regulatory requirements into the design process, ensuring that all aspects of the system meet the necessary standards from the outset.
  - **Benefit**: Reduces the risk of non-compliance and the need for costly redesigns or adjustments later in the project.

- **Thorough Documentation and Testing**: Detailed documentation and extensive testing are crucial for demonstrating compliance with safety and environmental regulations.
  - **Benefit**: Ensures that the system meets all regulatory requirements and facilitates smoother certification processes.

Resulting Benefits:

- **Enhanced Safety and Reliability:** Rigorous compliance and testing contribute to higher safety standards and reliability of the final system.
- **Faster Certification**: Effective compliance management can speed up the certification process through an evidence-generation process.

Leveraging Technological Advancements

Using systems engineering, we are able to harness technological advancements and integrate them effectively to enhance full system performance and capabilities.

Key Strategies:

- **Adoption of Emerging Technologies**: Engineers stay abreast of the latest technologies and integrate them into systems, such as advanced materials, AI, and additive manufacturing.
  - **Benefit**: Incorporates cutting-edge technologies that improve performance, efficiency, and innovation.

- **Technology Integration Frameworks**: Structured frameworks and methodologies for integrating new technologies ensure that they complement existing systems and operate as intended.
  - **Benefit**: Ensures smooth integration and maximises the benefits of new technologies without disrupting existing systems.

Resulting Benefits:

- **Enhanced System Performance**: The incorporation of advanced technologies leads to improved system performance, including better efficiency, capabilities, and user experience.
- **Innovation and Competitiveness**: Staying at the forefront of technological advancements keeps systems competitive and aligned with industry trends.

Optimising Safety and Reliability

Effective systems engineering places a strong emphasis on safety and reliability, employing rigorous analysis and testing to ensure that systems operate safely and reliably under all conditions.

Key Strategies:

- **Robust Failure Analysis**: Engineers conduct comprehensive FMEA and FTA to identify potential failure modes and implement preventive measures.
  - **Benefit**: Reduces the likelihood of failures and enhances the overall reliability of the system.

- **Reliability Testing and Validation**: Extensive testing, including simulation and field tests, ensures that systems perform reliably throughout their lifecycle.
  - **Benefit**: Validates system performance and reliability, ensuring that it meets or exceeds safety standards.

Resulting Benefits:

- **Higher Reliability:** Enhanced reliability leads to better operational performance and fewer unexpected issues.

Streamlining Supply Chain and Manufacturing

Systems engineering incorporates strategies to streamline supply chain and manufacturing processes, ensuring timely delivery and high-quality production.

Key Strategies:

- **Effective Supply Chain Management**: Engineers use advanced supply chain management practices to coordinate with suppliers, manage inventory, and ensure timely delivery of components.
  - **Benefit**: Minimises disruptions and ensures that production schedules are met.
- **Lean Manufacturing Techniques**: Implementing lean manufacturing principles helps to optimise production processes, reduce waste, and improve efficiency.
  - **Benefit**: Reduces production costs and improves overall manufacturing quality.

Resulting Benefits:

- **Efficient Production**: Streamlined processes and effective supply chain management lead to timely and cost-effective production.
- **High-Quality Outputs**: Enhanced manufacturing techniques ensure high-quality components and systems.

Chapter Conclusion

When systems engineering is applied correctly, and I do not mean by the letter but instead tailored to fit the system, it effectively addresses the challenges faced by **any** industry. By implementing structured processes, managing costs, ensuring compliance, integrating new technologies, focusing on safety and reliability, and optimising supply chain and manufacturing, systems engineering can overcome obstacles and realise significant benefits. These benefits include improved system performance, enhanced safety, cost efficiency, and timely delivery, and less rework throughout the development and use, ultimately contributing to the success and advancement of **any** system.

Remember that the principles and methods are to help you develop the system not to govern you. The most powerful tool in systems engineering's arsenal are questions. Especially:

- what do you want to achieve?
- why are you doing this? and
- who is it for?

6 EMERGING TRENDS AND THE FUTURE

Systems engineering is undergoing rapid evolution, driven by advances in technology, societal demands, and environmental concerns. As we look toward the future, several key trends are shaping the way systems are designed, developed, and operated. These trends are not only influencing the technical methodologies but also changing the landscape of the industry itself.

In this chapter, we explore the emerging trends in systems engineering, examining how new technologies and approaches are transforming the field. We will discuss each trend in detail, making sure both engineers and non-engineers can appreciate their significance and impact.

Digital Twins and Advanced Simulation

A Digital Twin is a virtual representation of a physical system, product, or process. It allows engineers to simulate, test, and analyse real-world performance without the need for physical prototypes. Digital Twins are fast becoming a fundamental tool throughout the lifecycle of a system, from initial design to maintenance and eventual decommissioning.

Digital Twins combine real-time data, historical data, and advanced simulation models to create a dynamic, virtual version of the physical system. This virtual system can be used to predict performance, identify potential failures, and optimise operations. For example, a digital twin of an aircraft engine can simulate how it will perform under different weather conditions or flight profiles, allowing engineers to adjust before issues arise. It can also run simulations faster than real-world testing so something that traditionally took weeks can now be carried out over a few hours.

By implementing Digital Twins engineers can explore multiple design variations and test their performance in real-world scenarios without having to build each one physically, significantly reducing development costs and time. Digital Twins enable risk-free experimentation, allowing designers to test extreme conditions or failure modes without risking damage to actual hardware. Then throughout the system lifecycle predictive maintenance becomes more efficient as Digital Twins allow engineers to foresee potential wear and tear on components before they fail.

Artificial Intelligence and Machine Learning

Artificial Intelligence (AI) and Machine Learning (ML) are transforming systems engineering by providing new ways to optimise design, enhance decision-making, and automate complex tasks. These technologies enable systems to learn from data, improving their performance over time without explicit programming. AI is powering the development of autonomous vehicles such as unmanned drones, boats, cars, and assembly lines that can navigate, make decisions, and perform tasks with minimal human intervention. For example, parcel delivery companies have been trialling various ways to deliver to customers without the interaction of humans. Some use drones to deliver medicine others use small, automated vehicles.

Machine learning algorithms are being used to optimise the design of components or processes. This can be either engineering or business optimisation and is done by analysing vast amounts of data so that these algorithms can identify patterns, unnecessary processes, and flaws in the system and suggest more efficient designs or processes that a human might overlook. For example, AI systems automatically suggest improved workflows based on past performance data, reducing the time to complete a task and improving quality.

Using AI models in the business where the AI system can handle repetitive and time-consuming tasks, allows engineers to focus on more creative and complex problem-solving. Another benefit of AI systems is that they can process large amounts of data in real time, allowing for faster and more accurate decision-making at critical moments. It is worth noting here though that as with all software programs the output is only as good as the programming and data entry. AI training takes a long time and is extremely repetitive for the human that is training the system.

Sustainability and Green Engineering

As the world faces increasing environmental challenges, sustainability is becoming a central focus in systems engineering. For example, developing green aerospace involves designing aircraft to reduce their environmental impact, primarily through lower emissions, energy efficiency, and the use of sustainable materials. Electric aircraft and hybrid propulsion systems are gaining traction as an alternative to traditional fuel-based engines. These systems produce fewer emissions and are quieter, making them more environmentally friendly, but they need systems engineering due to the complexity of replacing the traditional systems with the new ones whilst all the time still integrating with the older systems on board that will not be changed. It is not a case of simply changing an engine. Several companies are developing electric-powered aircraft for short-haul flights, which could drastically reduce the aviation industry's carbon footprint. To go with this, the manufacturers are investigating Biofuels and

Sustainable Aviation Fuel (SAF). Biofuels, made from renewable resources, offer a way to reduce greenhouse gas emissions from aircraft without requiring major changes to existing aircraft designs. SAF is a blend of traditional jet fuel and biofuels that reduces lifecycle emissions. Airlines have begun testing SAF on commercial flights, demonstrating that biofuels can be integrated into existing fleets with minimal disruption.

Combined with the engines and biofuel, manufacturers are constantly researching and developing lighter and lighter materials. For example, the use of advanced composite materials and lightweight metals can reduce the weight of aircraft, leading to improved fuel efficiency and lower emissions. Whilst materials are not strictly under the banner of systems engineering, it is the impact on the system that is of interest. New materials all need to perform as per the requirements and in some cases may need to be certified to be allowed to be used.

With these introductions engineers must now consider the entire lifecycle of a system, from raw material sourcing to end-of-life disposal, ensuring that each stage minimises environmental impact. The shift toward electric and hybrid propulsion requires new approaches to energy storage, battery technology, and the wider infrastructure, necessitating changes in design and operational methodologies.

Collaborative Engineering and the Use of Cloud Technologies

With globalisation and increasing complexity in any system, collaboration between teams has become essential. Cloud computing and collaborative engineering platforms are enabling engineers, designers, and stakeholders from different locations to work together in real-time, sharing data, models, and designs seamlessly. Engineering has become a truly global capability and on more than one occasion I have been developing requirements in the UK, then a team in Canada designed the systems, with the product prototype finally being tested in the US.

Cloud systems not only get used for the pure design of the product but also facilitate the management of vast amounts of data generated by modern systems, including voice communications, performance data, and maintenance records. These systems can be accessed by multiple teams and organisations, improving transparency and collaboration with the customers and other suppliers as needed. Collaborative engineering allows for faster design iterations, as engineers can simultaneously work on different aspects of a system without the delays caused by geographical separation. Cloud-based systems can easily scale to accommodate large projects, ensuring that even the most complex systems can be developed efficiently and effectively.

Using cloud-based systems bring a whole new problem in the implementation of cyber security and it is the role of systems engineering to include that in its systems thinking from the start. It used to be a bolt-on afterthought but as the technical world evolves it is now becoming a critical part of the system.

Autonomous and Unmanned Systems

Autonomous systems, such as Unmanned Ground-based Vehicles (UGVs), drones and Unmanned Aerial Vehicles (UAVs), are becoming a significant part of the transport landscape. These systems can operate without human control, opening new possibilities for exploration, transportation, and military applications. Companies are currently developing air taxis that are born out of the personal drone theories. These are new aerospace systems that have never been developed, regulated, flown, etc. before.

As such systems engineering is extremely important in the industry as they not only try to develop the full system but investigate how it will operate and fit into the current infrastructure and social society.

UAVs are being used for a variety of applications, from military operations to medical aid delivery and environmental monitoring. These systems can be controlled remotely or operated autonomously using AI and advanced sensors. For example, there are currently maritime vessels navigating the Oceans looking at climate change impact or cleaning up plastic reefs without any human interaction. As I have already mentioned, AI systems are being integrated into these UAVs to both navigate an optimised route but also to assess in rapid time any data from sensors. For example, UAVs are being used more and more to assess natural disasters and even to search for survivors, where time is critical.

Autonomous systems are critical for space exploration missions where real-time human control is impossible. These systems can make decisions, perform tasks, and adapt to changing conditions without direct human input. In my lifetime, we have gone from space travel being possible due to the space shuttle, which was mostly manual to rockets that now take off, navigate space, and then land back on earth on a platform on the sea, all without any human interaction. This will become more critical as we move towards Mars and beyond.

What this shows us is that engineers must now focus on integrating AI and machine learning algorithms into systems, as we used to say in the military 'fitted with' not 'fitted for', ensuring that these systems can operate independently and make decisions in real-time. These systems require specialised sensors, communication links, and control systems, leading to new design methodologies and testing procedures. Plus, as autonomous systems become more widespread, regulatory frameworks must evolve to ensure their safe operation in airspace and space environments.

Chapter Conclusion

The future of systems engineering is shaped by these emerging trends, which are fundamentally transforming how systems are designed, built, and operated. From Digital Twins and AI to sustainability and new technologies, the methodologies of the future will be more efficient, collaborative, and environmentally conscious. As these trends continue to evolve, engineers will need to adapt their approaches, ensuring that they remain at the forefront of technological innovation while addressing the challenges of an ever-changing world.

7 CONCLUSION & OUTLOOK

As we conclude this brief overview of systems engineering, and yes this really is brief as it is an extraordinarily complex subject, it is essential to reflect on the key insights gained and consider how the field will continue to evolve. This last chapter synthesises the concepts discussed throughout the book, emphasising how effective systems engineering practices address challenges and deliver substantial benefits. We will also look ahead to the future of systems engineering, highlighting areas of potential growth and innovation.

Recap of Systems Engineering Principles

Systems engineering is a multidisciplinary field that focuses on the design, development, and management of complex systems. For the final time in this book, I will repeat that, in my opinion, there is no such thing as a systems engineer. Even customers will ask for requirements engineers, verification engineers, design engineers, etc. If you say you are a systems engineer, then there is a strong possibility that they will struggle to understand what it is you do. What I will say is that the methodologies discussed in this book, including system design and analysis, architecture, optimisation, integration, and lifecycle management, provide a comprehensive framework for tackling the complexities of technical projects.

Probably the most encompassing method is that of the Systems Engineering Lifecycle. Remember, this is the structured approach to managing the entire lifecycle of a system, from concept through to decommissioning, ensuring that systems are developed efficiently and effectively. By adhering to these principles, systems engineers can address the inherent challenges of the field and deliver systems that meet the highest standards of performance, safety, and reliability.

Addressing Challenges through Systems Engineering

The challenges faced in systems engineering—such as complexity, cost, regulatory compliance, technological integration, safety, and supply chain management—require targeted strategies to overcome. Effective systems engineering practices provide solutions to these challenges:

- Complexity Management: Structured processes and tools like Model-Based Systems Engineering (MBSE) help manage the complexity of integrating numerous subsystems and components.

- Cost Control: Efficient design, prototyping, and lifecycle cost management practices ensure that projects remain within budget while delivering value.

- Regulatory Compliance: Integrating compliance requirements into the design process and maintaining thorough documentation facilitate meeting stringent safety and environmental standards.

- Technological Integration: Adopting and integrating new technologies through structured frameworks ensures that advancements enhance system performance without disrupting existing operations.

- Safety and Reliability: Comprehensive failure analysis, reliability testing, and preventive measures enhance the safety and reliability of complex systems.

- Supply Chain Optimisation: Effective supply chain management and lean manufacturing practices streamline production and ensure high-quality outputs.

These strategies not only address challenges but also position systems engineering to realise significant benefits, including improved system performance, cost efficiency, and timely delivery.

The Benefits of Effective Systems Engineering

When systems engineering is done correctly, the benefits are far-reaching:

- Enhanced Performance: Advanced design and optimisation techniques lead to superior performance in systems, including improved efficiency, capabilities, and reliability.

- Cost Savings: Effective management of design, prototyping, and lifecycle costs ensures that projects are cost-effective and provide good value for investment.

- Increased Safety: Rigorous compliance with safety standards and thorough reliability testing contribute to higher safety levels for users, operators, and other technology.

- Innovation and Competitiveness: Integration of new technologies and innovative practices keeps systems at the cutting edge of technology advancement, maintaining competitiveness in rapidly evolving industry applications.

- Efficient Production: Streamlined supply chain and manufacturing processes reduce production times and costs, leading to high-quality outputs.

These benefits highlight the importance of applying systems engineering principles effectively, ensuring that systems meet or exceed expectations while addressing complex challenges.

The Future of Systems Engineering

The future of systems engineering promises continued evolution and innovation. Several trends and emerging areas are likely to shape the field in the coming years:

- Increased Automation and Autonomy: Advancements in AI and machine learning will lead to greater automation and autonomy in systems, including autonomous aircraft and spacecraft.

- Sustainability Focus: Growing emphasis on environmental impact will drive innovations in green technologies, such as electric propulsion and sustainable aviation fuels.

- Advanced Manufacturing Techniques: Additive manufacturing (3D printing) and other advanced manufacturing methods will further transform production processes, enabling more complex and customised designs.

- Enhanced Collaboration: Cloud-based technologies and collaborative engineering platforms will facilitate more efficient teamwork and data sharing across global teams.

- Digital Twins and Real-Time Analytics: The use of Digital Twins and real-time analytics will become more prevalent, allowing for more accurate simulations, predictive maintenance, and optimised operations.

These advancements will continue to push the boundaries of what is possible in systems engineering, driving progress and innovation in industry.

A Brief Look at Systems Engineering

Systems engineering is a dynamic and multifaceted field that plays a crucial role in the development of advanced systems. By understanding and applying the principles and methodologies outlined in this book, engineers and other stakeholders can effectively address the challenges of complexity, cost, compliance, and safety. The benefits of effective systems engineering are substantial, leading to enhanced performance, cost savings, and innovation.

As the field continues to evolve, embracing emerging trends and technologies will be key to staying at the forefront of systems engineering. The future holds exciting possibilities, and the continued advancement of systems engineering will drive progress in industry, delivering new capabilities and opportunities across all industries no matter how large or small.

My final thought is if you take away anything from this book, I suggest that it is the following:

Systems engineering is not the goal. It is simply a tool in your toolbox to allow you to design, develop, and use technology whilst reducing the risk that it will go wrong. Most projects do go wrong at some point but if you don't implement systems engineering early the cost of fixing the issue is a lot higher both in value and reputation. If you are managing a complex engineering project never underestimate the value of a good "systems engineer"

A Brief Look at Systems Engineering

ABOUT THE AUTHOR

Mark is an accomplished engineer having spent 30 years working on both aerospace and defence projects across the full systems engineering lifecycle. He started his career as an airman in the Royal Air Force where he learnt to maintain the aircraft.

Now Mark works in the civilian aerospace sector developing the next generation of aircraft in what is called Urban Air Mobility. He is passionate about the cross-transfer of this engineering subset to almost any application or industry sector as well as having developed a technology integration framework process.

Mark is available as a consultant to talk through all things systems engineering and the application of its tools and methodologies into any technology or domain. Should you wish to engage Mark then contact:

mark.gilbert@gmx.es

Printed by Amazon Italia Logistica S.r.l.
Torrazza Piemonte (TO), Italy